PIANO • VOCAL • GUITAR

2nd Edition

THE DEFINITIVE
Love
COLLECTION

100 Songs

ISBN 0-7935-3624-3

HAL•LEONARD®
CORPORATION
7777 W. BLUEMOUND RD. P.O. BOX 13819 MILWAUKEE, WI 53213

Visit Hal Leonard Online at
www.halleonard.com

THE DEFINITIVE
Love
COLLECTION

ALL I ASK OF YOU
from THE PHANTOM OF THE OPERA

Music by ANDREW LLOYD WEBBER
Lyrics by CHARLES HART
Additional Lyrics by RICHARD STILGOE

No more talk of dark-ness, for-get these wide-eyed fears: I'm

here, noth-ing can harm you, my words will warm and calm you.

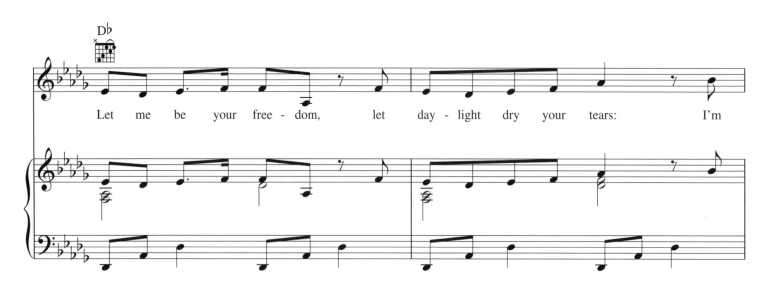

Let me be your free-dom, let day-light dry your tears: I'm

ALWAYS ON MY MIND

Words and Music by WAYNE THOMPSON,
MARK JAMES and JOHNNY CHRISTOPHER

ALL MY LOVING

Words and Music by JOHN LENNON
and PAUL McCARTNEY

ALL THE THINGS YOU ARE

from VERY WARM FOR MAY

Lyrics by OSCAR HAMMERSTEIN II
Music by JEROME KERN

ALWAYS

Words and Music by
IRVING BERLIN

AND I LOVE HER

Words and Music by JOHN LENNON
and PAUL McCARTNEY

I give her all my love,
She gives me ev-'ry-thing
Bright are the stars that shine,

that's all I do.
and ten-der-ly.
dark is the sky.

AND I LOVE YOU SO

Words and Music by
DON McLEAN

ANNIVERSARY SONG

from the Columbia Picture THE JOLSON STORY

By AL JOLSON
and SAUL CHAPLIN

Oh! how we danced on the night
night seemed to fade in - to blos -

we were wed. We vowed our true
- som - ing dawn. The sun shone a -

love though a word was - n't said.
new but the dance lin - gered on.

THE ANNIVERSARY WALTZ

Words and Music by AL DUBIN
and DAVE FRANKLIN

We just dis - cov - ered each oth - er _____ to - night when the

lights were low. _____ One dance led up to an -

oth - er, _____ and now I can't let you go, so:

THE BLUE ROOM
from THE GIRL FRIEND

Words by LORENZ HART
Music by RICHARD RODGERS

CALL ME IRRESPONSIBLE

from the Paramount Picture PAPA'S DELICATE CONDITION

Words by SAMMY CAHN
Music by JAMES VAN HEUSEN

CAN'T HELP FALLING IN LOVE

from the Paramount Picture BLUE HAWAII

Words and Music by GEORGE DAVID WEISS,
HUGO PERETTI and LUIGI CREATORE

CHEEK TO CHEEK
from the RKO Radio Motion Picture TOP HAT

Words and Music by
IRVING BERLIN

Heav - en, _____ I'm in Heav - en. _____ And my

heart beats so that I can hard - ly speak. _____ And I

(They Long to Be)
CLOSE TO YOU

Lyric by HAL DAVID
Music by BURT BACHARACH

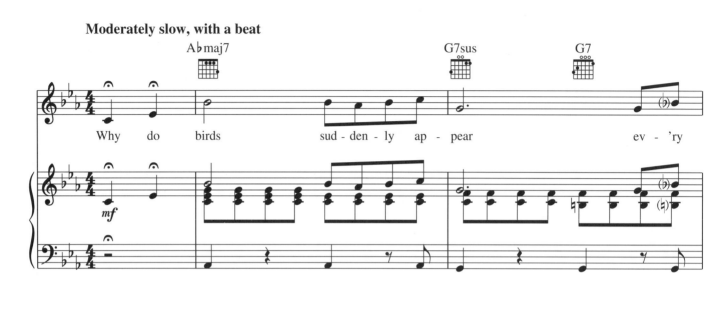

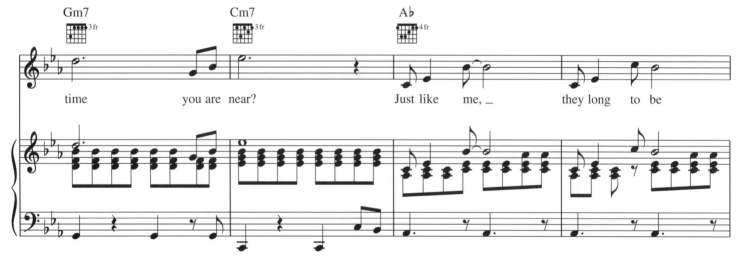

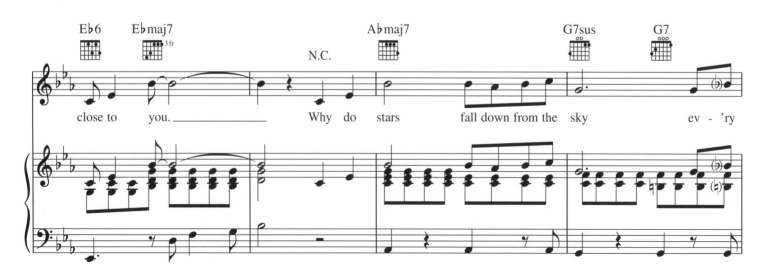

COME RAIN OR COME SHINE

from ST. LOUIS WOMAN

Words by JOHNNY MERCER
Music by HAROLD ARLEN

COULD I HAVE THIS DANCE

Words and Music by WAYLAND HOLYFIELD
and BOB HOUSE

I'll al-ways re-mem-ber the song they were
al-ways re-mem-ber that mag-ic

play-ing, the first time _____ we danced and I knew.
mo-ment, when I held _____ you close to me.

As we swayed to the mu-sic _____ and held to each
As we moved to-geth-er, _____ I knew for-

DAY BY DAY

Theme from the Paramount Television Series DAY BY DAY

Words and Music by SAMMY CAHN,
AXEL STORDAHL and PAUL WESTON

ENDLESS LOVE

Words and Music by
LIONEL RICHIE

My love, there's on-ly you in my life,
Two hearts, two hearts that beat as one;
the on-ly thing that's right.
our lives have just be-gun.
My
For-
first love,
ev- er,
you're ev-'ry breath that I take,
I'll hold you close in my arms,

Oh, _____ and __ love, _____

ETERNALLY
from LIMELIGHT

Words and Music by CHARLES CHAPLIN
and GEOFFREY PARSONS

Slowly, with great feeling

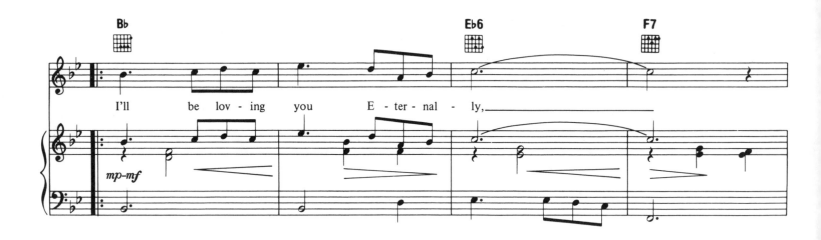

I'll be lov-ing you E-ter-nal-ly,

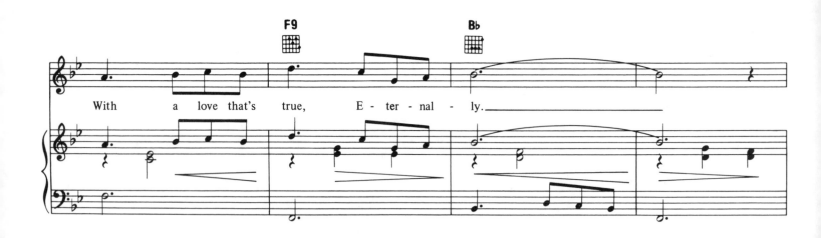

With a love that's true, E-ter-nal-ly.

(I Love You)
FOR SENTIMENTAL REASONS

Words by DEEK WATSON
Music by WILLIAM BEST

FOR ME AND MY GAL

Words by EDGAR LESLIE and E. RAY GOETZ
Music by GEORGE W. MEYER

THE GIRL THAT I MARRY

from the Stage Production ANNIE GET YOUR GUN

Words and Music by
IRVING BERLIN

THE GLORY OF LOVE

from GUESS WHO'S COMING TO DINNER

Words and Music by
BILLY HILL

HAVE I TOLD YOU LATELY

Words and Music by
VAN MORRISON

A GROOVY KIND OF LOVE

Words and Music by TONI WINE
and CAROLE BAYER SAGER

HAVE I TOLD YOU LATELY
THAT I LOVE YOU

Words and Music by
SCOTT WISEMAN

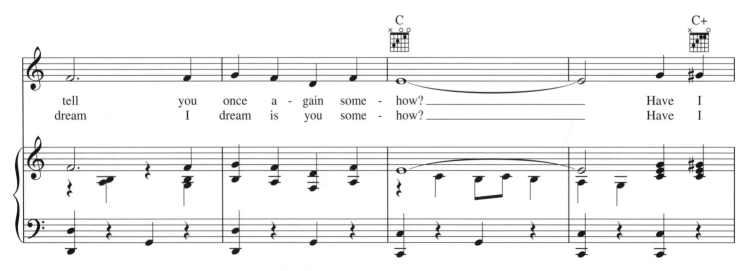

THE HAWAIIAN WEDDING SONG
(Ke Kali Nei Au)

English Lyrics by AL HOFFMAN and DICK MANNING
Hawaiian Lyrics and Music by CHARLES E. KING

Slowly, with much warmth

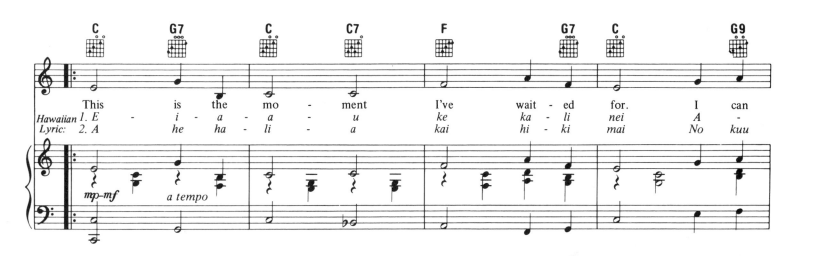

This   is the mo - ment   I've wait - ed for.   I can

Hawaiian 1. E - i - a - a - u   ke   ka - li   nei   A -

Lyric: 2. A he ha - li - a   kai   hi - ki   mai   No kuu

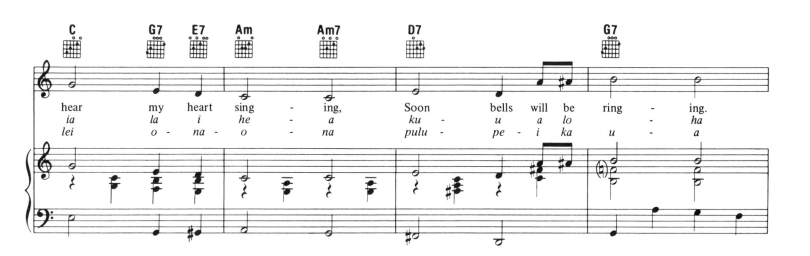

hear my heart sing - ing,   Soon bells will be ring - ing.

ia la i   he - a   ku - u a lo - ha

lei o - na - o - na   pulu - pe - i ka u - a

HEART AND SOUL
from the Paramount Short Subject A SONG IS BORN

Words by FRANK LOESSER
Music by HOAGY CARMICHAEL

HELLO, YOUNG LOVERS
from THE KING AND I

Lyrics by OSCAR HAMMERSTEIN II
Music by RICHARD RODGERS

Refrain *(very moderately)*

HOW DEEP IS THE OCEAN
(How High Is the Sky)

Words and Music by
IRVING BERLIN

I HONESTLY LOVE YOU

Words and Music by PETER ALLEN
and JEFF BARRY

Lyrics:

May-be I hang a-round __ here a lit-tle more than I should; we
You don't __ have to an-swer; I see it in your eyes.

both know I got some-where else __ to go. But
May-be it was bet-ter left __ un-said. But

I HAVE DREAMED

from THE KING AND I

Lyrics by OSCAR HAMMERSTEIN II
Music by RICHARD RODGERS

A - lone and a - wake, I've looked at the stars, the same that smiled on you. _____ And

I LOVE HOW YOU LOVE ME

Words and Music by BARRY MANN
and LARRY KOLBER

I LOVE YOU

from MEXICAN HAYRIDE

Words and Music by
COLE PORTER

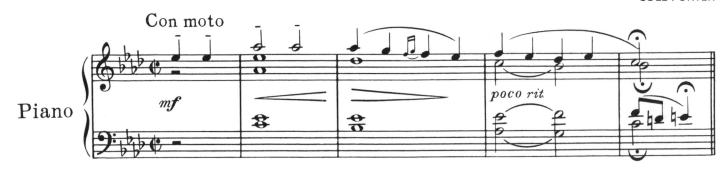

If a love song I could on-ly write,_____ A song with words and

mu-sic di-vine_____ I would ser-e-nade you ev-'ry

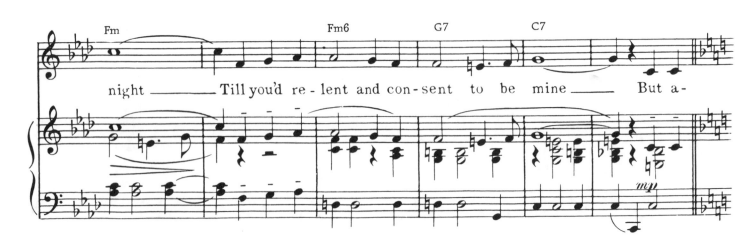

night_____ Till you'd re-lent and con-sent to be mine_____ But a-

ISN'T IT ROMANTIC?

from the Paramount Picture LOVE ME TONIGHT

Words by LORENZ HART
Music by RICHARD RODGERS

I LOVE YOU TRULY

Words and Music by
CARRIE JACOBS-BOND

Andante con amore

I WANNA BE LOVED

Words by BILLY ROSE and EDWARD HEYMAN
Music by JOHN GREEN

I WANT YOU, I NEED YOU, I LOVE YOU

Words by MAURICE MYSELS
Music by IRA KOSLOFF

I'M WISHING

Words by LARRY MOREY
Music by FRANK CHURCHILL

I'VE GOT MY LOVE TO KEEP ME WARM

from the 20th Century Fox Motion Picture ON THE AVENUE

Words and Music by
IRVING BERLIN

Bright jump tempo

IF

Moderately, with feeling

Words and Music by
DAVID GATES

IT COULD HAPPEN TO YOU

from the Paramount Picture AND THE ANGELS SING

Words by JOHNNY BURKE
Music by JAMES VAN HEUSEN

JUNE IN JANUARY
from the Paramount Picture HERE IS MY HEART

Words and Music by LEO ROBIN
and RALPH RAINGER

feel the scent of ros - es in the air. It's

June in Jan - u - ar - y be - cause I'm in

love, but on - ly be - cause I'm in love with

you. _____ It's you. _____

JUST THE WAY YOU ARE

Words and Music by
BILLY JOEL

the way you are.

D.S. al Coda

CODA

Solo ends I don't want clev-er

con - ver - sa - tion; I nev-er

LADY IN RED

Words and Music by
CHRIS DeBURGH

THE LAST WALTZ

Words and Music by LES REED
and BARRY MASON

LET ME CALL YOU SWEETHEART

Words by BETH SLATER WHITSON
Music by LEO FRIEDMAN

LET'S FALL IN LOVE

Words by TED KOEHLER
Music by HAROLD ARLEN

LITTLE GIRL

Words and Music by MADELINE HYDE
and FRANCIS HENRY

Dad - dy used to tell __ me __ if I ran too fast I'd fall and hurt __
home, there stands an old __ house __ with a pick - ett fence be - neath the big __

my - self. __
oak tree.

But the
I can

LONG AGO
(And Far Away)
from COVER GIRL

Words by IRA GERSHWIN
Music by JEROME KERN

Drear - y days are o - ver; life's a four-leaf clo - ver.

Ses - sions of de - pres - sions are through. _____ Ev - 'ry

hope I longed for long a - go comes true. _____

THE LOOK OF LOVE

from CASINO ROYALE

Words by HAL DAVID
Music by BURT BACHARACH

LONGER

Words and Music by
DAN FOGELBERG

L-O-V-E

Words and Music by BERT KAEMPFERT
and MILT GABLER

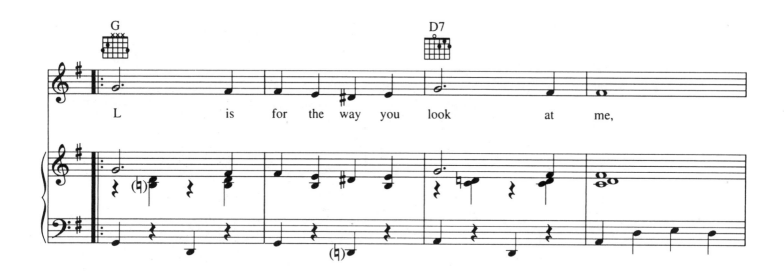

L is for the way you look at me,

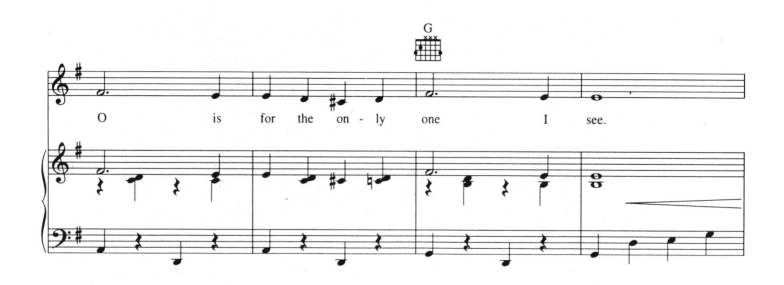

O is for the on-ly one I see.

LOVER
from the Paramount Picture LOVE ME TONIGHT

Words by LORENZ HART
Music by RICHARD RODGERS

LOVE LETTERS
Theme from the Paramount Picture LOVE LETTERS

Words by EDWARD HEYMAN
Music by VICTOR YOUNG

LOVE ME DO

Words and Music by JOHN LENNON
and PAUL McCARTNEY

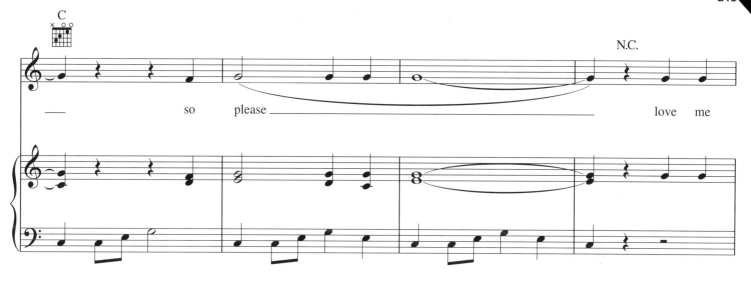

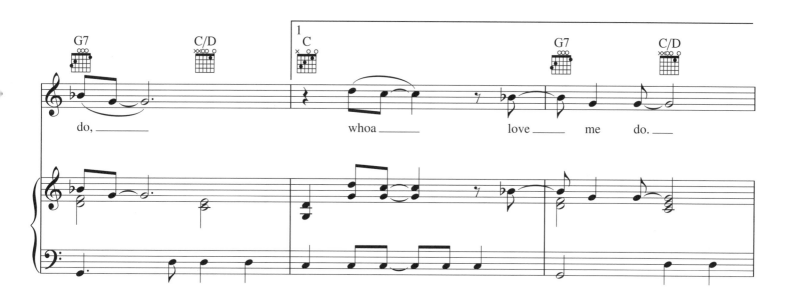

LOVE ME TENDER

Words and Music by ELVIS PRESLEY
and VERA MATSON

Moderately slow

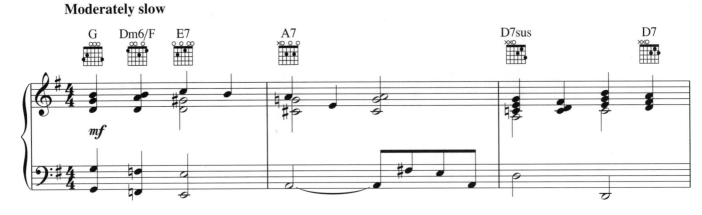

Love me ten - der, love me sweet,
Love me ten - der, love me long,
Love me ten - der, love me dear,
When at last my dreams come true,

nev - er let me go.
take me to your heart,
tell me you are mine.
dar - ling, this I know:

You have made my
for it's there that
I'll be yours through
Hap - pi - ness will

(You've Got)
THE MAGIC TOUCH

Words and Music by
BUCK RAM

You've got the mag - ic touch, _____ it makes me glow so much; _____ it casts a spell, _____ it rings a bell, the mag - ic touch; _____ Oh, when I

MAKE IT WITH YOU

Words and Music by
DAVID GATES

MEMORIES ARE MADE OF THIS

Words and Music by RICHARD DEHR,
FRANK MILLER and TERRY GILKYSON

MOONLIGHT BECOMES YOU

from the Paramount Picture ROAD TO MOROCCO

Words by JOHNNY BURKE
Music by JAMES VAN HEUSEN

MY FUNNY VALENTINE
from BABES IN ARMS

Words by LORENZ HART
Music by RICHARD RODGERS

THE NEARNESS OF YOU

from the Paramount Picture ROMANCE IN THE DARK

Words by NED WASHINGTON
Music by HOAGY CARMICHAEL

MY HEART STOOD STILL

from A CONNECTICUT YANKEE

Words by LORENZ HART
Music by RICHARD RODGERS

B♭6 C7 F Gm7 C7 F G♯dim7
3fr
heart stood still! My feet could
Gm7 C7 F F+ Gm7 C7
3fr
3fr
step and walk, My lips could move and talk,
F F+ B♭6 C7 F B♭6 F
And yet my heart stood still! Though not a
Fm C+ C
sin - gle word was spok - en, I could tell you knew, That un - felt

MY ROMANCE
from JUMBO

Words by LORENZ HART
Music by RICHARD RODGERS

A NIGHTINGALE SANG IN BERKELEY SQUARE

Lyric by ERIC MASCHWITZ
Music by MANNING SHERWIN

Slowly

When true lov-ers meet in May-fair, so the leg-ends tell, song birds sing, win-ter turns to spring, ev-'ry wind-ing street in May-fair falls be-neath the spell. I

*Pronounced "Bar-kley"

POLKA DOTS AND MOONBEAMS

Words by JOHNNY BURKE
Music by JIMMY VAN HEUSEN

NO OTHER LOVE

from ME AND JULIET

Lyrics by OSCAR HAMMERSTEIN II
Music by RICHARD RODGERS

ONE DOZEN ROSES

Words by ROGER LEWIS and "COUNTRY" JOE WASHBURN
Music by DICK JURGENS and WALTER DONOVAN

ONE SONG

Words by LARRY MOREY
Music by FRANK CHURCHILL

THE POWER OF LOVE

Words by MARY SUSAN APPLEGATE and JENNIFER RUSH
Music by CANDY DEROUGE and GUNTHER MENDE

Slowly, with a steady beat

The whis - pers ___ in the morn - ing ___ of lov-ers sleep - ing tight are roll - ing by ___ like thun - der now,

PRECIOUS AND FEW

Words and Music by
WALTER D. NIMS

Pre-cious and few ___ are the mo - ments we two can share.
Ba - by it's you ___ on my mind, ___ your love is so rare.

Qui - et and blue ___ like the sky ___
Be - ing with you ___ is a feel -

___ I'm hung o - ver you. ___
- ing I just can't com - pare. ___

And if I
And if I

And if I can't find my way back home ___

it just would-n't be fair, ___ 'cause pre-cious and few ___ are the mo-

- ments we two can share.

Pre-cious and few ___ are the mo - ments we two can share. ___

T YOUR HEAD ON MY SHOULDER

Words and Music by
PAUL ANKA

Put your head on my should - er, Hold me in your arms, Ba - by.

Squeeze me oh so tight, Show me that you love me too. ___

___ Put your lips close to mine, dear. Won't you kiss me once, Ba - by?

REMEMBER

Words and Music by
IRVING BERLIN

SAVE THE BEST FOR LAST

Words and Music by PHIL GALDSTON,
JON LIND and WENDY WALDMAN

SO IN LOVE

from KISS ME, KATE

Words and Music by
COLE PORTER

love with you, my love _____ am

SOME ENCHANTED EVENING

from SOUTH PACIFIC

Lyrics by OSCAR HAMMERSTEIN II
Music by RICHARD RODGERS

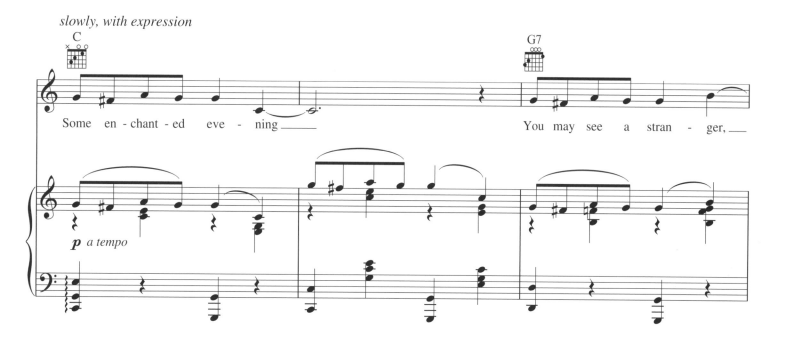

SOME DAY MY PRINCE WILL COME

Words by LARRY MOREY
Music by FRANK CHURCHILL

SOMEWHERE OUT THERE

from AN AMERICAN TAIL

Words and Music by JAMES HORNER,
BARRY MANN and CYNTHIA WEIL

through, then we'll be to-geth - er some-where out there, out

where dreams come true.

TEARS IN HEAVEN

Words and Music by ERIC CLAPTON
and WILL JENNINGS

Would you know my name _____
Would you hold my hand _____
Would you know my name _____

if I saw you in heav - en?
if I saw you in heav - en?
if I saw you in heav - en?

Would it be the same _____
Would you help me stand _____
Would you be the same _____

Be - yond the door _____ there's peace, I'm sure, _____

SPEAK SOFTLY, LOVE
(Love Theme)
from the Paramount Picture THE GODFATHER

Words by LARRY KUSIK
Music by NINO ROTA

THAT'S AMORÉ
(That's Love)
from the Paramount Picture THE CADDY

Words by JACK BROOKS
Music by HARRY WARREN

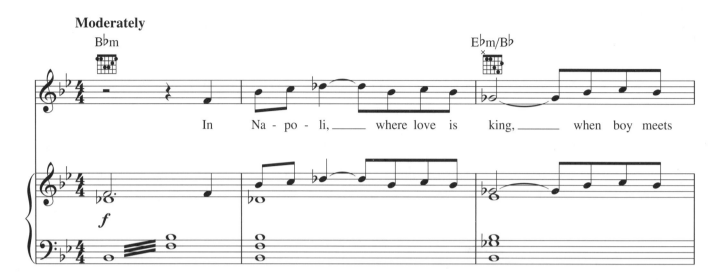

A TIME FOR US
(Love Theme)
from the Paramount Picture ROMEO AND JULIET

Words by LARRY KUSIK and EDDIE SNYDER
Music by NINO ROTA

Slowly and expressively

A time for us some-day there'll be when chains are torn by cour-age born of a love that's free. A time when dreams so long de-

thorns   we will en - dure   as we pass sure - ly through ev - 'ry

storm.   A time for us   some - day there'll be _____ a

new   world, _____ a world   of   shin - ing

hope   for   you   and   me.   A   time   for   me.

THEY SAY IT'S WONDERFUL

from the Stage Production ANNIE GET YOUR GUN

Words and Music by
IRVING BERLIN

THROUGH THE YEARS

Words and Music by STEVE DORFF
and MARTY PANZER

TO EACH HIS OWN

from the Paramount Picture TO EACH HIS OWN
from the Paramount Picture THE CONVERSATION

Words and Music by JAY LIVINGSTON
and RAY EVANS

TONIGHT, I CELEBRATE MY LOVE

Music by MICHAEL MASSER
Lyric by GERRY GOFFIN

Slowly and expressively

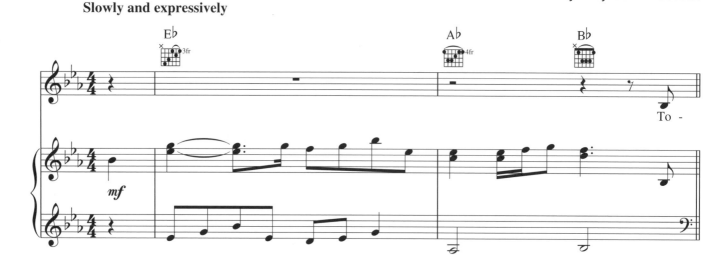

To -

night ____ I cel - e - brate my love ____ for you; ____ it seems ____ the nat - u - ral
night ____ I cel - e - brate my love ____ for you; ____ and hope ____ that deep in - side you
night ____ I cel - e - brate my love ____ for you; ____ and soon ____ this old world will

thing ____ to do. To - night ____ no one's gon - na find us, ____ we'll leave the world ____ be -
feel ____ it too. To - night ____ our spir - its will be climb - ing to a sky lit up ____ with
seem ____ brand new. To - night ____ we will both dis - cov - er ____ how friends turn in - to

TRUE LOVE
from HIGH SOCIETY

Words and Music by
COLE PORTER

TWO SLEEPY PEOPLE

from the Paramount Motion Picture THANKS FOR THE MEMORY

Words by FRANK LOESSER
Music by HOAGY CARMICHAEL

UNFORGETTABLE

Words and Music by
IRVING GORDON

UP WHERE WE BELONG

from the Paramount Picture AN OFFICER AND A GENTLEMAN

Words by WILL JENNINGS
Music by BUFFY SAINTE-MARIE and JACK NITZSCHE

Who knows what to-mor-row brings; in a world, few hearts sur-vive? All I know is the way I feel; when it's real, I keep it a-live.

Some hang on to "used to be," live their lives look-ing be-hind. All we have is here and now; all our life, out there to find.

The

THE WAY YOU LOOK TONIGHT

from SWING TIME

Words by DOROTHY FIELDS
Music by JEROME KERN

WHAT A DIFF'RENCE A DAY MADE

English Words by STANLEY ADAMS
Music and Spanish Words by MARIA GREVER

WHAT YOU WON'T DO FOR LOVE

Words and Music by BOBBY CALDWELL
and ALFONS KETTNER

WHEN I FALL IN LOVE

Words by EDWARD HEYMAN
Music by VICTOR YOUNG

YOU NEEDED ME

Words and Music by
RANDY GOODRUM

Moderately

WHERE DO I BEGIN

(Love Theme)

from the Paramount Picture LOVE STORY

Words by CARL SIGMAN
Music by FRANCIS LAI

A WHOLE NEW WORLD

(Aladdin's Theme)
from Walt Disney's ALADDIN

Music by ALAN MENKEN
Lyrics by TIM RICE

YOU ARE SO BEAUTIFUL

Words and Music by BILLY PRESTON
and BRUCE FISHER

Moderately slow, expressively

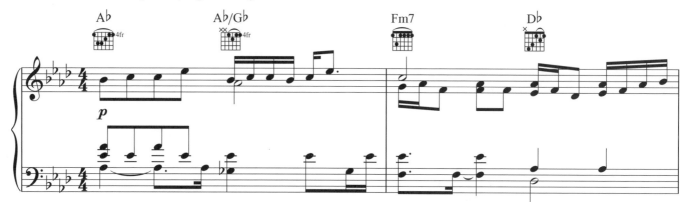

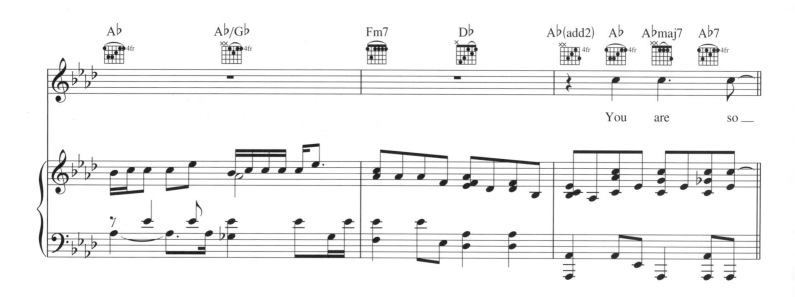

You are so ____

____ beau - ti - ful ____   to

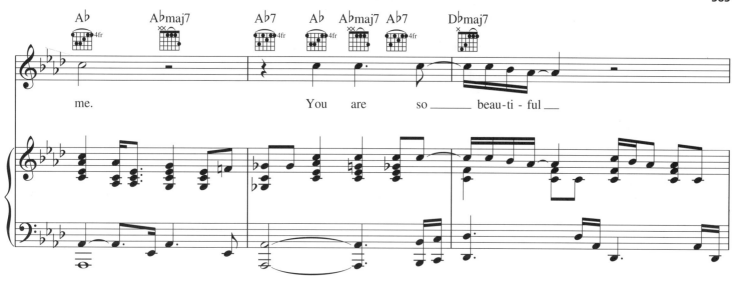

me. You are so ___ beau-ti - ful ___

to me. Can't you

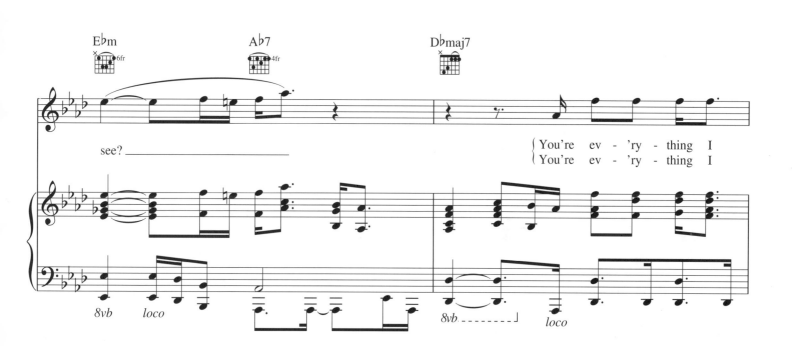

see? ___

You're ev - 'ry - thing I
You're ev - 'ry - thing I

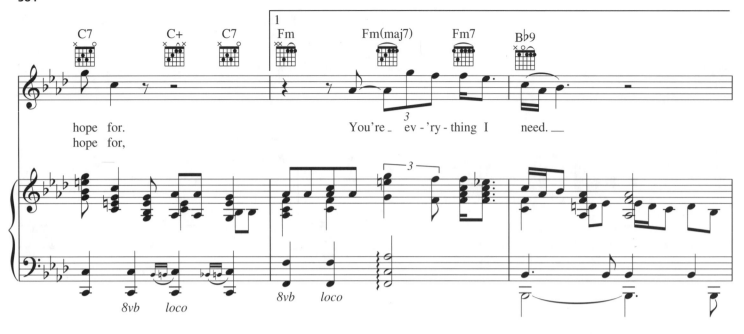

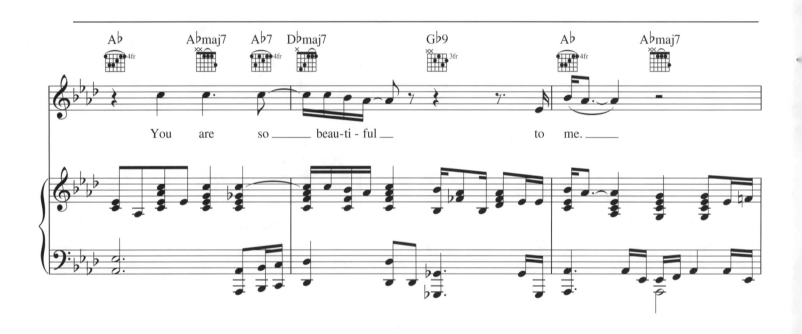

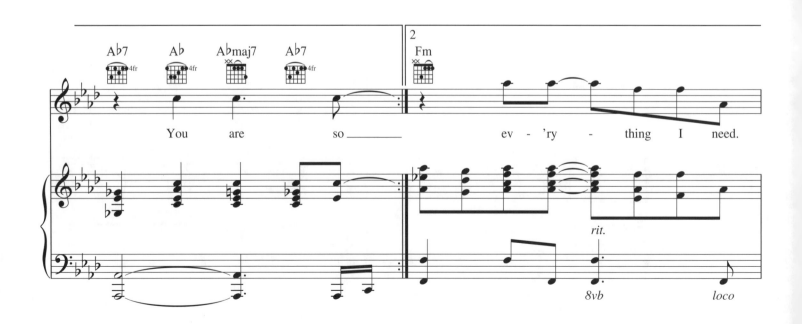

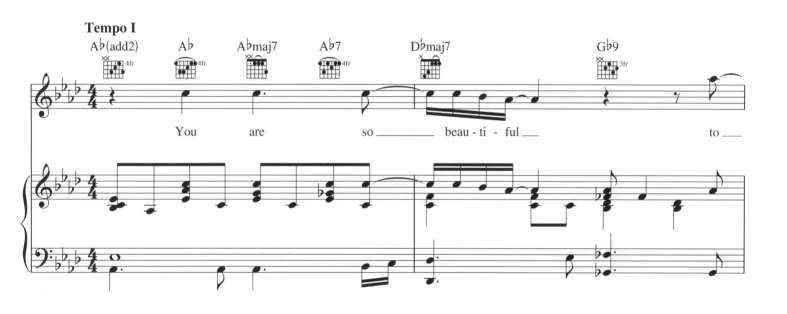

You are so _____ beau - ti - ful _____ to _____

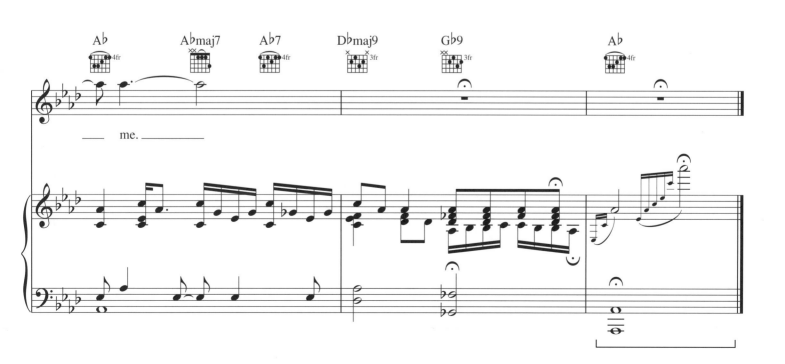

_____ me. _____

YOU'VE GOT A FRIEND

Words and Music by
CAROLE KING

Moderately

When you're down _____ and trou - bled and you
a - bove _____ you should turn

need a help - ing hand _____ and noth - ing, whoa,
dark and full of clouds _____ and that old north

noth - ing is go - ing right, _____
wind should be - gin _____ to blow, _____

*Vocal harmony sung 2nd time only

THE DEFINITIVE COLLECTIONS

These magnificent folios each feature a quintessential selection of songs. Each has outstanding piano/vocal arrangements showcased by beautiful full-color covers. Books are spiral-bound for convenience and longevity.

The Definitive Blues Collection

A massive collection of 96 blues classics. Songs include: Baby, Won't You Please Come Home • Basin Street Blues • Everyday (I Have the Blues) • Gloomy Sunday • I'm a Man • (I'm Your) Hoochie Coochie Man • Milk Cow Blues • Nobody Knows You When You're Down and Out • The Seventh Son • St. Louis Blues • The Thrill Is Gone • and more.
00311563 ....$29.95

The Definitive Broadway Collection

142 of the greatest show tunes ever compiled into one volume, including: Don't Cry for Me Argentina • Hello, Dolly! • I Dreamed a Dream • Lullaby of Broadway • Mack the Knife • Memory • Send in the Clowns • Somewhere • The Sound of Music • Sunrise, Sunset • Tomorrow • What I Did for Love • more.
00359570 ....$29.95

The Definitive Christmas Collection

An authoritative collection of 126 Christmas classics, including: Blue Christmas • The Chipmunk Song • The Christmas Song (Chestnuts Roasting) • Feliz Navidad • Frosty the Snow Man • Happy Hanukkah, My Friend • Happy Holiday • (There's No Place Like) Home for the Holidays • O Come, All Ye Faithful • Rudolph, the Red-Nosed Reindeer • Tennessee Christmas • more!
00311602 ....$29.95

The Definitive Classical Collection

129 selections of favorite classical piano pieces and instrumental and operatic literature transcribed for piano. Features music by Johann Sebastian Bach, Ludwig van Beethoven, Georges Bizet, Johannes Brahms, Frederic Chopin, Claude Debussy, George Frideric Handel, Felix Mendelssohn, Johann Pachelbel, Franz Schubert, Johann Strauss, Jr., Pyotr Il'yich Tchaikovsky, Richard Wagner, and many more!
00310772 ....$29.95

The Definitive Country Collection

A must-own collection of 101 country classics, including: Coward of the County • Crazy • Daddy Sang Bass • Forever and Ever, Amen • Friends in Low Places • God Bless the U.S.A. • Grandpa (Tell Me About the Good Old Days) • Help Me Make It Through the Night • I Was Country When Country Wasn't Cool • I'm Not Lisa • I've Come to Expect It from You • I've Cried My Last Tear for You • Luckenbach, Texas • Make the World Go Away • Mammas Don't Let Your Babies Grow Up to Be Cowboys • Okie from Muskogee • Tennessee Flat Top Box • Through the Years • Where've You Been • and many more.
00311555 ....$29.95

The Definitive Dixieland Collection

Over 70 Dixieland classics, including: Ain't Misbehavin' • Alexander's Ragtime Band • Basin Street Blues • Bill Bailey, Won't You Please Come Home? • Dinah • Do You Know What It Means to Miss New Orleans? • I Ain't Got Nobody • King Porter Stomp • Shreveport Stomp • When the Saints Go Marching In • and more.
00311575 ....$29.95

The Definitive Hymn Collection

An amazing collection of over 200 treasured hymns, including: Abide with Me • All Glory, Laud and Honor • All Things Bright and Beautiful • At the Cross • Battle Hymn of the Republic • Be Thou My Vision • Blessed Assurance • Church in the Wildwood • Higher Ground • How Firm a Foundation • In the Garden • Just As I Am • A Mighty Fortress Is Our God • Nearer, My God, to Thee • The Old Rugged Cross • Rock of Ages • Sweet By and By • Were You There? • and more.
00310773 ....$29.95

The Definitive Jazz Collection

90 of the greatest jazz songs ever. including: Ain't Misbehavin' • All the Things You Are • Birdland • Body and Soul • Girl from Ipanema • The Lady Is a Tramp • Midnight Sun • Moonlight in Vermont • Night and Day • Skylark • Stormy Weather • Sweet Georgia Brown.
00359571 ....$29.95

The Definitive Love Collection – 2nd Edition

100 sentimental favorites! Includes: All I Ask of You • Can't Help Falling in Love • Endless Love • The Glory of Love • I've Got My Love to Keep Me Warm • Isn't It Romantic? • Love Me Tender • Save the Best for Last • So in Love • Somewhere Out There • Unforgettable • When I Fall in Love • You Are So Beautiful • more.
00311681 ....$24.95

The Definitive Movie Collection – 2nd Edition

A comprehensive collection of over 100 songs that set the moods for movies, including: Alfie • Beauty and the Beast • Blue Velvet • Can You Feel the Love Tonight • Easter Parade • Endless Love • Forrest Gump Suite • Theme from Jurassic Park • My Heart Will Go On • The Rainbow Connection • Someday My Prince Will Come • Under the Sea • Up Where We Belong • and more.
00311705 ....$29.95

The Definitive Rock 'n' Roll Collection – 2nd Edition

A classic collection of the best songs from the early rock 'n' roll years – 1955-1968. 95 songs, including: Barbara Ann • Chantilly Lace • Dream Lover • Duke of Earl • Earth Angel • Great Balls of Fire • Louie, Louie • Rock Around the Clock • Ruby Baby • Runaway • (Seven Little Girls) Sitting in the Back Seat • Stay • Surfin' U.S.A. • Wild Thing • Woolly Bully • and more.
00490195 ....$29.95

Prices, contents and availability subject to change without notice.

FOR MORE INFORMATION, SEE YOUR LOCAL MUSIC DEALER, OR WRITE TO:

HAL•LEONARD® CORPORATION

7777 W. BLUEMOUND RD. P.O. BOX 13819 MILWAUKEE, WI 53213